learn it
live it
BIBLE STUDIES™

SPIRITUAL DISCIPLINES

Group
Loveland, Colorado

Group's R.E.A.L. Guarantee to you:

This Group resource incorporates our R.E.A.L. approach to ministry—one that encourages long-term retention and life transformation. It's ministry that's:

Relational
Because learner-to-learner interaction enhances learning and builds Christian friendships.

Experiential
Because what learners experience through discussion and action sticks with them up to 9 times longer than what they simply hear or read.

Applicable
Because the aim of Christian education is to equip learners to be both hearers and doers of God's Word.

Learner-based
Because learners understand and retain more when the learning process takes into consideration how they learn best.

Learn It, Live It Bible Studies™: Spiritual Disciplines
Copyright © 2003 Group Publishing, Inc.

Visit our Web site: **www.grouppublishing.com**

Credits
Contributors: Stacey T. Campbell, Matt Lockhart, G. Brenton Mock, Ken and Lori Niles, and Larry Shallenberger
Editor: Beth Rowland
Development Editor: Matt Lockhart
Chief Creative Officer: Joani Schultz
Copy Editor: Alison Imbriaco
Art Director: Randy Kady
Print Production Artist: Susan Tripp
Cover Art Director: Jeff A. Storm
Cover Designer: Toolbox Creative
Cover Photographer: Daniel Treat
Production Manager: Dodie Tipton

Unless otherwise noted, Scripture taken from the HOLY BIBLE, NEW INTERNATIONAL VERSION®. Copyright © 1973, 1978, 1984 by International Bible Society. Used by permission of Zondervan Publishing House. All rights reserved.

ISBN 0-7644-2670-2

10 9 8 7 6 5 4 3 2 1   12 11 10 09 08 07 06 05 04 03

Printed in the United States of America.

Table of Contents

Introduction to Group's
Learn It, Live It Bible Studies™

Welcome to an exciting new concept in small-group Bible studies! At Group, we recognize the value of Bible study to Christian growth—there's no better way to grow in our faith than to study the living Word of God. We also know the value of group activity. Activity helps us practice what we learn. And this is vital to the Christian faith. Jesus doesn't tell us simply to learn about him, he asks us to become like him in thoughts, in words, and in actions. That's why Group developed *Learn It, Live It Bible Studies*. In these studies, you'll be challenged not only to learn more about God but also to put what you've learned into practice in a powerful and meaningful way.

Whether you're new to Bible study or a seasoned pro, you'll find the Bible study to be interesting and compelling. In the Bible study section of each lesson, you'll open God's Word with the others in your group. You'll study relevant Scripture passages and discuss thought-provoking questions that will help you all grow in your faith and in your understanding of who God is and what he wants for your lives.

After the Bible study, you'll be invited to choose a group project that will help you practice the very thing you've just learned. Some of these projects are simple, easy, and low-risk. Others will require a greater commitment of time and resources; they may even take you beyond your comfort zone. But whichever group project you choose to do, you can be certain that it will help you grow more like Christ in your everyday life.

We hope you enjoy these lessons! And we pray that by studying these lessons and doing these projects that you'll find yourself becoming more and more like our Lord Jesus Christ.

Spiritual Disciplines

This seven-session Bible study focuses on spiritual disciplines. Many Christians are wary of spiritual disciplines, fearing that they are strange, mystical, and unbiblical. However, the spiritual disciplines covered in these Bible courses are simply behaviors that all Christians should practice regularly as part of their Christian faith.

These habits of the Christian faith help us focus our attention on God and on being his disciples. Notice the similarity between the word *disciple* and the word *discipline*. To be a disciple is to lead a disciplined life, faithfully and habitually following the teachings of the Master. To practice the spiritual disciplines is to go beyond acquiring knowledge about God and faith and to live the Christian live with zest and zeal.

When we pray, study, fast, serve, steward our resources, worship, and rest regularly, we will experience remarkable growth and increased depth in our spiritual lives. We will find ourselves understanding God and his purposes more fully. We will find that we feel ourselves to be more attuned to God's presence and to his plan for us. We will find that our love for God grows beyond anything we could imagine. And we will also find that following Christ, and living the Christian life, will become more natural, more joyful, and more fulfilling.

About the Sessions

Start It *(15 minutes)*

This part of the lesson is designed to introduce everyone to the day's topic and to get discussion flowing. Here you'll find an introduction to read and a quick warm-up to do together.

Study It *(45-60 minutes)*

This is the Bible study portion of the lesson. Every lesson provides several Scripture passages to look up and nine to twelve discussion questions for you to talk over as a group. Feel free to jot down your insights in the space provided.

You'll also notice that each lesson includes extra information in the margins. You'll find Bible facts, definitions, and quotations. Please note that the information doesn't always come from a Christian perspective. These margin notes are meant to be thought-provoking and get your group discussing each topic at a deeper level.

Close It *(15-30 minutes)*

During the Close It section of the lesson, you'll do two things. First, you'll read through the Live It options at the end of the lesson and choose one to do together as a group. You'll find more information about the Live It options in the next section.

Second, you'll pray together as a group. Be sure to take the time to listen to one another's prayer requests. You may want to write those prayer requests in the space provided so you can pray for them throughout the week. Don't rush your time with God. Praying with others is a precious opportunity. Make the most of it!

Part 2: live it

In each lesson in this study, you'll find five Live It options. These group activities are designed to help your Bible study group live out what you learned in the Bible study. Together as a group, you'll read over the Live It options each week. Then choose one to do together. You'll find that some of the activities are quick and easy and can be done without planning an extra session. Other activities will require more time and planning. Some activities are very low-risk. Others might push group members to the edge of their comfort zone. Some of the activities are suitable for partici- pation by entire families. Others will work better if you arrange for child care. Choose the option that interests your group the most and carry it out. You'll find that you learn so much more when you practice it in real life.

Prayer

To seasoned prayer warriors, there is nothing more rewarding than spending hours in intense conversation with God. But to the rest of us, prayer can be a mysterious and intimidating practice. We wonder what we're supposed to say. We wonder whether God is listening, because he seems so silent. We wonder whether our prayers really move the hand of an all-knowing and all-powerful God.

Many Christians struggle to make a daily practice of prayer that's more than asking God's blessing at mealtime. It's a tough discipline. After all, it's hard to keep talking when the other one in the conversation doesn't audibly respond. But prayer can be one of the most rewarding and profitable ways to spend our time. The Bible tells us that we can boldly approach the throne of God. Scripture also tells us to bring all our requests, all our worries, all our problems to God. What a magnificent privilege! Prayer helps us connect with God in the same way that a phone call, an e-mail, or a chat over coffee connects us with a friend. Through prayer we can discern the will of God, we can have victory over temptation, and we can find healing for our hurts. By praying, we renew our friendship with God.

This small-group experience will allow you to investigate what the Bible says about how to pray. As you study and practice, you will strengthen your conversational skills with God and find peace and fulfillment that can only be found through a relationship with God.

Part 1: *learn it*

Start It *(15 minutes)*
Conversation Kindling

> **Leader:** Because this is the start of a new study series (or perhaps it's the first meeting of your small group), take the opportunity to help group members discuss their expectations for the series and the relationships in the group. You might want to consider having your group draft a list of expectations for the group, such as attendance and how long the meeting should be.

To start the session, choose one or two of the following questions to answer. Share your answers with the group.

- What type of person do you find easy to talk with and be friends with?

- How easy is it to have a friendly and conversational relationship with God? Explain.

- What do you find hardest and easiest about prayer?

Study It *(45-60 minutes)*

> If you have a large group, form smaller groups of four to seven people to answer the discussion questions. At the end of the Study It section, allow time for the subgroups to report to the whole group.

1. In what ways is prayer a spiritual discipline?

Read Matthew 6:9-13.

    2. What elements does Jesus identify as important in prayer? Why do you think Jesus included these elements? Is there anything Jesus did not include that surprises you? Explain.

Read Matthew 7:7-11.

    3. Why do you think it is important to remember to approach prayer in the context of a relationship between a child and a father?

Read the note about Mary Magdalene de' Pazzi. Also read Matthew 6:5-8.

4. What is your reaction to Mary Magdalene de' Pazzi's perspective on prayer? What attitudes are appropriate or inappropriate when we pray?

Read I Thessalonians 5:17.

5. Is praying continually a realistic expectation? How do we get to the point where we are in constant communication with God?

6. Form pairs or trios and divide these passages among you. Read your verses, and note what you learn about prayer. After a few minutes, summarize your verses, and share your insights with the entire group.

- *Mark 1:35; Luke 6:12-13*
- *Luke 18:1-8*
- *2 Corinthians 1:10-11*
- *Ephesians 6:18*

- *Philippians 4:6-7*
- *Colossians 4:12*
- *1 Timothy 2:1-4*
- *Hebrews 4:14-16*

Read the margin note about Bill Hybels.

7. What is your reaction to Bill Hybels' questions? What questions could you make a habit of asking God? Why is it important to listen to God?

In the book *Too Busy Not to Pray*, pastor Bill Hybels wrote about developing a custom set of questions to ask God. He offers three questions, which he regularly asks God:
• What's the next step in developing my character?
• What's the next step in my family?
• What's the next step in my ministry?

8. How does prayer affect us? our relationship with God? our relationships with others? the world around us?

9. What keeps us from a disciplined life of prayer? What can you do to put aside those things that hinder your prayer life?

10. What changes can you make in your life that might help you practice the spiritual discipline of prayer better?

Close It (15-30 minutes)

Review the options in the Live It section of this session and make plans as a group to complete one of these activities prior to moving on to the next section. This is your opportunity to move from theory to practice—*carpe diem!*

Pray It

Share prayer requests and close in prayer. Be sure to ask God to guide your efforts as you plan and carry out a Live It activity.

Plan It

What activity are we going to do?

When are we going to do this?

Where will this activity take place?

Other: Specific instructions/my responsibility

Option 1

As a group, pray through ACTS (**a**doration, **c**onfession, **t**hanksgiving, **s**upplication). Write the letters A, C, T, and S across the top of a large piece of newsprint. As a group, brainstorm things to pray about that fall under these four categories. Have a recorder write all your prayer ideas under the appropriate column. Use your piece of newsprint as a reminder to pray for all of the things your group came up with. Then pray together, going through each category.

Option 2

Praying at regular times throughout the day has been part of many Christian traditions for centuries. In fact, the custom goes back to the Jews in Bible times (see Psalm 119:164). The custom has grown over the years into a practice called "fixed-hour prayer," "Praying the Hours" or praying "the Divine Office."

Spend at least one day this week praying the hours. There are online sources that will help you know the official prayers for each hour of a specific day. Check out www.universalis.com. You may also want to use *The Book of Common Prayer* or one of the books in Phyllis Tickle's series *The Divine Hours*. (She's written a book for spring prayers, one for summer prayers, and another for fall and winter prayers.)

Or you can simply pray at these intervals during the day:

Lauds: when you wake up
Prime: when you get out of bed
Terce: mid-morning (9 a.m.)
Sext: noon
Nones: mid-afternoon (3 p.m.)
Vespers: early evening (6 p.m.)
Compline: bedtime

Option 3

Choose prayer partners in the group. You may want to have women pray with women and men pray with men. Each pair will choose a time to pray together over the telephone for five minutes each day. Use these times as opportunities to share specific prayer requests. Change prayer partners the next time your group meets. You can continue this activity indefinitely.

Option 4

One of the time-honored practices of the church is praying Scripture. Choose a favorite passage of Scripture, or use Psalm 23, Psalm 51, or John 17. Individually, write the first verse of the passage you choose on a sheet of paper. Pause to reflect on its meaning. Then write a prayer to God based on how God speaks to you through this verse. Continue writing each verse, reflecting on it, and writing a prayer until you've prayed your way through the entire passage. Then share insights as a group.

Option 5

Prayer is not just talking to God; it is also listening to God. Hold a "listening day" as a group. Meet at your church or at a quiet, wooded park. Spend the first hour praying and worshipping as a group. Then have everyone go to a quiet place to be alone with God. Each person may bring a Bible, a devotional, a notebook, and a pen. Spend three hours in prayer, reading Scripture, and quietly waiting for God to speak. Write anything that you believe God is saying to you in the notebook. Share a meal together and talk about what you believe God has said to you.

Debrief It

After experiencing this session's Live It activity, discuss these questions as a group:

- **On a scale of 1 (low) to 10 (high), how would you rank your experience? Why?**

- **What was the most important insight you gained from this experience?**

- **How can you incorporate this spiritual discipline into your life regularly?**

Journal It

The following space is provided for you to record your personal thoughts, reflections, impressions, or feelings about this session's topic and Live It activity.

Study

The word *study* probably brings to mind long evenings with a boring textbook and the anxiety of cramming for tests in school. Very few people would claim to truly enjoy studying. However, as a spiritual discipline, study can be a richly rewarding experience.

To study as a spiritual discipline is to purposefully learn about God and about the Christian faith. It's something that many Christians do on a regular basis. We listen to the sermon at church; we listen to Christian radio; we read our Bibles during personal devotional times; we attend Bible studies. Study may in fact be the spiritual discipline that Christians are most familiar with and most comfortable with because learning is so highly valued among church leaders.

However, true study is more than simply taking in information. As Christians we do not want to have minds stuffed to bursting with trivial Bible facts. Our learning has a very high purpose: We seek to know and love God and to learn how to serve him better.

This Bible study will help you understand how, why, and what we are to study. Then you'll be able to choose an activity to help you put your newfound knowledge into practice and make learning a vital and exciting part of your Christian walk.

Part 1: *learn it*

Start It *(15 minutes)*

Remember It Well

Choose something from your pockets or your purse to put on the floor in the middle of the room. If you don't have anything, ask your host if you can use something from the room, such as a book or a vase. If you have fewer than seven people in your group, have everyone put in two items.

Together, study the items for thirty seconds. Then turn your back to the items, and list them to see if you can remember them all. Compare your results to everyone else's.

Then discuss these questions:

- **Was it easy or hard for you to remember all these items? Explain.**

- **Did studying the items help you remember them? Why or why not?**

- **What does it take to really learn about, remember, and understand something?**

- **Is studying something you enjoy? Why or why not?**

Study It *(45-60 minutes)*

If you have a large group, form smaller groups of four to seven people to answer the discussion questions. Allow time at the end of the Study It section for the subgroups to report to the whole group.

1. In what ways is study a spiritual discipline?

2. How does God teach us? What place does study have in that?

Read Jeremiah 15:16.

3. Do you find study to be natural and joyous? Why or why not?

Read John 8:31-32 and Colossians 3:16.

4. What's the goal when we study?

learn it

live it

Read Psalm 119:27; Romans 12:2; and Philippians 4:8.

5. How can the spiritual discipline of study help us follow the counsel of these verses?

6. As Christians, what are we to study? How are we to study?

7. What keeps us from studying? How can we avoid those things?

8. Form pairs or trios and divide these passages among you. Read your verses, and note what you learn about study. After a few minutes, summarize your verses, and share your insights with the entire group.

- *Deuteronomy 11:18-19*
- *Job 23:12*
- *Psalm 119:11*
- *Hosea 4:6*

- *Luke 11:28*
- *Acts 17:11*
- *Romans 15:4*
- *2 Timothy 3:14-17*

Read the margin note. Also read Hebrews 5:11-14.

9. What cautions do we need to be aware of as we strive to undertake the discipline of study?

10. What can you do to better practice this spiritual discipline?

Close It *(15-30 minutes)*

Review the options in the Live It section of this session, and make plans as a group to complete one of these activities prior to moving into the next section. This is your opportunity to move from theory to practice—*carpe diem!*

Pray It

Share prayer requests and close in prayer. Be sure to ask God to guide your efforts as you plan and carry out a Live It activity.

Plan It

What activity are we going to do?

When are we going to do this?

Where will this activity take place?

Other: Specific instructions/my responsibility

Part 2: live it

Option 1

Choose a time to meet when you'll have an hour and a half to study Scripture. Have someone type Psalm 1 with double-spaced lines and wide margins, and make a photocopy for each person.

Form study groups of two or three. Begin your time together by committing it to God, asking him to make his Word come alive to you. Then divide the rest of the time in this way:

Spend fifteen minutes individually observing as many facts as you can discover about this passage. Then spend ten minutes discussing those facts within your small study group.

Spend the next fifteen minutes working alone, reviewing the facts and asking the following questions. Then write a one-sentence summary of the basic truth of the passage.

• Why did the author structure the passage this way?
• Are there key words or repetitions that stand out?
• What is the main point the author wants to communicate?

Spend ten minutes discussing your discoveries with your group.

Spend the next fifteen minutes working alone, considering how the passage applies to your life. Write action steps you believe God wants you to take. Then spend the next ten minutes sharing your discoveries and plans with your group. Pray together.

Don't forget this last step: Be sure to immediately put into practice the action steps you wrote!

Option 2

Commit to studying the book of 1 John together this week. For the next five days, study one chapter from the book each day. Spend at least half an hour reading the chapter, studying it, praying over it, and learning all you can about it. Write down your discoveries as well as any questions you have. Gather to discuss what you've learned, to ask each other the questions you have, and to praise God for teaching you through his Word. Discuss together how the book of 1 John can transform the way you each live your lives. Make plans to put the teachings of 1 John into practice.

Option 3

Choose one verse of Scripture and meditate on it for the entire week. Study your verse carefully, reflect on its meaning, and pray it to God. You may want to keep a journal and write your thoughts about the verse in it. Try to focus on the verse several times a day. For example, think about the verse when you wake up, at work, as you eat your lunch, as you take a walk, or after you go to bed. Come together at the end of the week to discuss what you discovered.

Option 4

Together, choose one or several verses to memorize. Recite your verse or verses to yourself and at least one other person every day. Here are some verses you might like to memorize:
- *Romans 12:1-2*
- *2 Timothy 3:16-17*
- *Galatians 2:20*
- *Titus 3:4-5*
- *Colossians 3:12*

Option 5

Choose a classic Christian book to read together. You may want to read *The Cost of Discipleship* by Dietrich Bonhoeffer, *Mere Christianity* by C.S. Lewis, *Celebration of Discipline* by Richard Foster, *Knowing God* by J.I. Packer, or *The Pilgrim's Progress* by John Bunyan. Divide the chapters among the members of the group. Read your assigned chapter, and prepare a five- to ten-minute presentation. Meet together one night this week so that people can give their presentations.

Debrief It

After experiencing this session's Live It activity, discuss these questions as a group:

- **On a scale of 1 (low) to 10 (high), how would you rank your experience? Why?**

- **What was the most important insight you gained from this experience?**

- **How can you incorporate this spiritual discipline into your life regularly?**

Journal It

The following space is provided for you to record your personal thoughts, reflections, impressions, or feelings about this session's topic and Live It activity.

Fasting

In natural-health circles, fasting is touted as a way to cure everything from depression to cancer. Historically, fasting has been used to topple occupying governments and to protest oppressive regimes. Fasting is used in religions as diverse as Judaism, Hinduism, and the religions of the Native Americans. Yet, most Christians in the twenty-first century know little about the discipline and have never practiced it themselves.

However, the Bible seems to take it for granted that we would fast. Jesus didn't say, "If you fast..." or even, "Thou shalt fast." He said, "*When* you fast..." (Matthew 6:16). There are at least thirty references to fasting in Scripture. It's mentioned in at least twenty books of the Bible. Clearly, the practice of fasting deserves a closer look.

This lesson will give you the chance to study the Scriptures and take a careful look at the spiritual discipline of fasting. Through study and practice, you'll uncover how fasting can help you come to know God in a deeper and more satisfying way.

Part 1: *learn it*

Start It *(15 minutes)*
Feast or Famine?

To get started with today's lesson, choose one or two of the following questions to answer. Share your answer with the group.

- **What type of food most tempts you?**

- **When you hear the word *fasting*, what images or thoughts come to mind?**

- **Have you ever fasted before? If so, what was the experience like for you? If not, why?**

Study It *(45-60 minutes)*

If you have a large group, form smaller groups of four to seven people to answer the discussion questions. Allow time at the end of the Study It section for the subgroups to report to the whole group.

1. Fasting is mentioned in at least twenty books of the Bible. Why do you think that fasting is not talked about much or practiced much today?

2. Form pairs or trios and divide these passages among you. Read your verses, and note what you learn about fasting. After a few minutes, summarize your verses, and share your insights with the entire group.

- *Isaiah 58:3-9*
- *Daniel 1:8-16*
- *Joel 1:13-14; 2:12-15*
- *Zechariah 7:2-6*

- *Matthew 6:16-18; 9:14-15*
- *Acts 13:1-3; 14:23*
- *Colossians 2:20-23*

Read the quotation from Richard Foster.

3. How might fasting keep us from being enslaved by our cravings and desires?

"How quickly we crave things we do not need until we are enslaved by them. Paul wrote, ' "All things are lawful for me," but I will not be enslaved by anything' (1 Corinthians 6:12). Our human cravings and desires are like a river that tends to overflow its banks; fasting helps keep them in their proper channel."

Richard J. Foster, *Celebration of Discipline*

4. What misconceptions do people have about fasting? How would you respond to people who misunderstand fasting?

5. What should the purpose of a fast be? What are the benefits of fasting?

"When a person chooses fasting as a spiritual discipline, he or she must, then, practice it well enough and often enough to become experienced in it, because only the person who is well habituated to systematic fasting as a discipline can use it effectively as a part of direct service to God, as in special times of prayer or other service."

Dallas Willard, *The Spirit of the Disciplines*

Read the quotation from Dallas Willard.
6. Do you agree with Dallas Willard? How could regularly practicing the discipline of fasting benefit your relationship with God?

Read the information in the margin about biblical fasts.

7. What do you think are the important elements of practicing the spiritual discipline of fasting? Discuss both practical and spiritual elements.

Read Luke 18:9-14.

8. Regardless of the spiritual discipline (prayer, fasting, stewardship), what role does our motive or heart play in our coming before God?

Biblical Fasts

Partial Fast: A restriction of the diet. A fast of this type might be to restrict the diet to only raw fruits and vegetables. See Daniel 10:3.

Normal Fasting: Abstaining from food (including juices). Water is allowed in this type of fast. This fast can last up to forty days. See Luke 4:1-2.

Absolute Fast: Abstaining from all food and water. Without super-natural aid, this type of fast can last no longer than three days. See Esther 4:16.

In Scripture, fasting can be both a private, individual practice and a corporate practice. For example, all Jews were required to fast on the Day of Atonement.

9. If you were given a day especially dedicated to prayer and fasting, where would you like to spend that day and what might your agenda include?

Close It *(15-30 minutes)*

Review the options in the Live It section of this session and make plans as a group to complete one of these activities prior to moving onto the next session. This is your opportunity to move from theory to practice—*carpe diem!*

Pray It

Share prayer requests and close in prayer. Be sure to ask God to guide your efforts as you plan and carry out a Live It activity.

Plan It

What activity are we going to do?

When are we going to do this?

Where will this activity take place?

Other: Specific instructions/my responsibility

Part 2: live it

> **Note:** Some of these options call for fasting from food. If you have any medical conditions or are on any medications, check with your doctor prior to undertaking a fast. If you do choose to fast from food, be sure to keep yourself hydrated by drinking plenty of water rather than coffee or black tea.

Option 1

Commit as a group to fast from a meal together. Plan to meet as a group at that mealtime, and plan an agenda for the time. For example, you may want to spend the time in prayer and worship.

Option 2

> **Leader:** Have index cards or slips of paper available for this option.

As individuals, identify something you do on a daily basis that you feel would be beneficial to fast from for a period of time. You might want to consider watching TV, surfing the Web, eating dessert, drinking coffee, or drinking sodas. Once you have chosen something, write it on an index card and then tell the group what you wrote.

As a group, commit to fast together for an agreed-upon length of time, such as one week. Sign your card and swap it with an accountability partner. Tell your partner how he or she might best be able to encourage you and pray for you during your fast.

Option 3

As a group, select a day and fast together. One way to accomplish this is by fasting from morning until the evening meal. This will be a twenty-four-hour fast if you don't eat after the evening meal of the previous day. To fast from all three meals in one day (a thirty-six-hour fast) is probably too hard for a first try at fasting. If you are new to fasting, you may want to abstain from solid food but allow juice.

Plan to come together as a group to worship and eat dinner to break your fast. Be sure the meal is a simple one, such as veg-etable soup, fresh fruit, and bread. A large or heavy meal is difficult to digest after fasting.

Option 4

Some people find spiritual benefit from serving others while fasting. Choose a time your group can fast from a meal together while you serve others. You may want to serve a group that often faces hunger, such as the homeless. Make sure you approach the time of service prayerfully—use the time to commune with God and to seek him.

Option 5

Plan an extended fast with your group. You may choose to fast together on the same day of the week over a course of weeks or months. (This option will be easiest to accomplish if your group is new to fasting). Or you may choose a multi-day fast. In either case, agree to pray, worship, and seek God during your fast. Gather together regularly to share how fasting has changed your relationship with God.

Debrief It

After experiencing this session's Live It activity, discuss these questions as a group:

- **On a scale of 1 (low) to 10 (high), how would you rank your experience? Why?**

- **What was the most important insight you gained from this experience?**

- **How can you incorporate this spiritual discipline into your life regularly? How do you think it will affect your life?**

Journal It

The following space is provided for you to record your personal thoughts, reflections, impressions, or feelings about this session's topic and Live It activity.

Service

What do you think of when you hear the word *service*? A waiter in a fancy uniform with a towel draped over his arm? Someone who performs menial tasks? A slave? Or maybe you think of having to do something you know you *should* do but don't really want to do.

The spiritual discipline of service is something entirely different. Serving can help us understand and appreciate God more. It helps us love others as God wants us to love them. Serving helps us develop humility and compassion. It helps us appreciate Christ, who washed his disciples' feet, fed multitudes of hungry people, healed countless sick and hurting people, and sacrificed himself on the cross for our salvation.

Serving also helps us grow and live our faith more fully. The spiritual discipline of service is an important tool to help us become the people God designed us to be. As John Ortberg wrote in *The Life You've Always Wanted,* "When [growth] happens, I don't just *do* the things Jesus would have done; I find myself *wanting* to do them. They appeal to me. They make sense. I don't just go around trying to do right things; I *become* the right person."

In this session, you'll uncover several biblical examples of service, and you'll explore the impact those acts of service made. Then you'll have the opportunity to put what you've learned into practice in ways that could change both your life and the lives of others.

Part 1:  learn it

Start It *(15 minutes)*
Serve a Friend!

> Leader: Provide snacks and drinks for this meeting. Set them on a table near where the group will gather, but wait to serve them.

Begin today's Bible study by enjoying a snack together in this fun and unusual way. Take turns going to get a snack and a drink. The first person should bring back a snack and a drink and serve them to someone else. Then the person who received the snack and drink should go get a snack and drink to give to someone else. Continue until everyone in the group has been served. Then enjoy the snacks together. While you eat, talk about these things:

- **Tell the group about a time someone served you in a particularly meaningful way.**

- **What emotions does service evoke in you when you're the one being served? When you're the one serving?**

Study It *(45-60 minutes)*

> If you have a large group, form smaller groups of four to seven people to answer the discussion questions. At the end of the **Study It** section, allow time for the subgroups to report to the whole group.

1. In what ways is service a spiritual discipline?

Read the margin note and Ephesians 4:11-16.

> 2. Why do we serve? How do we serve? What is the result of our service?

Read Matthew 20:25-28 and Matthew 25:31-46.

3. What do these passages teach about service?

4. Why is service so important?

5. How does practicing the spiritual discipline of service affect us spiritually? How does it affect our relationship with God and others?

6. What keeps people from serving others?

Read Romans 7:6.

7. What's the difference between serving "in the new way of the Spirit" and serving "in the old way of the written code"? How does this affect your attitude and your actions?

Read Revelation 5:9-10.

8. What is *priestly* about service? Who are we to serve, ultimately? Explain.

9. Form pairs or trios and divide the following list of verses among you. Read your verses and note what you learn about service. After a few minutes, summarize your verses and share your ideas with the rest of the group.

   • *Matthew 5:14-16*
   • *Galatians 5:13-14*
   • *Galatians 6:9-10*
   • *Ephesians 6:7-8*
   • *1 Peter 4:10-11*

Read John 13:1-17.

10. What does Jesus' example teach us?

11. What can you do in your life to help you practice the spiritual discipline of service better?

Close It *(15-30 minutes)*

Review the options in the Live It section of this session, and make plans as a group to complete one of these activities prior to moving onto the next session. This is your opportunity to move from theory to practice—*carpe diem!*

Pray It

Share prayer requests and close in prayer. Be sure to ask God to guide your efforts as you plan and carry out a Live It activity.

Plan It

What activity are we going to do?

When are we going to do this?

Where will this activity take place?

Other: Specific instructions/my responsibility

Option 1

As a group, watch the movie, *Babette's Feast,* about a nineteenth century French refugee who lives with two elderly sisters in Denmark. To celebrate the one-hundredth anniversary of the birth of the sisters' late father—who had been the group's revered pastor—Babette convinces the sisters to let her be in charge of preparing a huge meal for the parish. She creates the feast of a lifetime, while at the same time demonstrating humility and servanthood to a group of people who have become petty and obsessed with bickering.

Afterward discuss what the film said to you about:

• what it means to serve others,
• the risks involved in serving others, and
• how the people being served might react.

Then choose a way to serve your community, even if those you serve don't deserve it, won't notice it, or won't appreciate it. You might serve a group whose political views don't match your own or a group of rebellious and troubled teens. You might clean up an area of your town that's run-down and crime-ridden, or you might offer to help local authorities clean up graffiti.

Option 2

Choose the neighborhood of someone in your group, and agree to serve the people who live there by washing the residents' cars. Pick a day and time, and make simple fliers to pass out to the neighbors, letting them know that your group will be washing cars. Let them know the location and the time of the event. Make sure it's clear that this is a free neighborhood service, with no strings attached.

On the day of the event, go door-to-door and let the neighbors know what you're doing. Invite them to bring their cars by for a free wash. Wash and dry each car thoroughly, but accept no donations. If anyone asks why you're doing the car wash, feel free to say something like, "Because of the good things God has done for us, we want to turn around and do good things for others."

Option 3

Gather together for a foot-washing service. Begin by sitting in a circle with warm water, soap, and towels close by. Choose someone to read John 13:1-17 aloud to the group. When everyone has removed shoes and socks, the first person should wash the next person's feet, putting the feet in the warm water one at a time, rubbing them gently, then removing them and drying them on a towel. Have the person whose feet were just washed wash the next person's feet. Continue around the circle until each person's feet have been washed.

This service can be done in silence, with worship music playing softly in the background, or you may all quietly remind each other of all that Jesus has done for us on the cross.

When everyone's feet have been washed, pray together. Commit yourselves to serving God, each other, the church, and the world around you. Be sure to thank God for all he's done for you.

Option 4

Put everyone's name in a hat and draw names. If members of your group are married, you may want to consider having the women draw women's names and the men draw men's names. Have each person do at least one act of service per day for the person whose name he or she drew. At the end of the week, gather and discuss what it was like to purposefully serve someone every day. How hard was it to remember? How hard was it to think of something every day? What insights does this activity give you about serving others?

Option 5

As a group, find a needy single mom, someone undergoing AIDS treatment, or someone else in your community who is in desperate need, and adopt the person for at least six months. If possible choose someone outside your church family. If no one in your group knows of such a person, contact your church or your local social services.

Care for the person and offer love to him or her. Be a friend, offering financial help, transportation, food, companionship, or whatever else is needed. Ask the person to join your group. If you feel led, ask the person to go to church with you, but remember: Your goal is not to get the person to church; your goal is to serve him or her with no obligations and no strings attached. If you have an ulterior motive such as getting the person to church, your acts of service might be seen as self-serving or manipulative. However if the person is not a Christian, be sensitive to God's leading and share the gospel with him or her if it's appropriate.

Debrief It

After experiencing this session's Live It activity, discuss these questions as a group:

- **On a scale of 1 (low) to 10 (high), how would you rank this experience? Why?**

- **What was the most important insight you gained from this experience?**

- **How can you incorporate this spiritual discipline into your life regularly?**

Journal It

The following space is provided for you to record your personal thoughts, reflections, impressions, or feelings about this session's topic and Live It activity.

Stewardship

Stewardship is a nearly defunct word in our culture. *Consumerism* is a more powerful descriptor of our society. We commonly use the Consumer-Confidence Index and consumer debt to measure the performance of the economy. We don't have a stewardship index.

Stewardship may be an unpopular concept in our culture, but God founded the first society on the concept of stewardship: God created a paradise and gave it to Adam and Eve to manage. While many well-churched people generally think of stewardship in terms of money, the biblical idea of stewardship is much broader. It captures the idea that Christians are to manage all of the gifts that God has given them.

This lesson will help your group better understand the privileges and responsibilities we have as stewards of our God-given resources.

Part 1: *learn it*

Start It *(15 minutes)*
House Manager

> **Leader:** Before your group meets, collect a baby doll, play money, and a ball cap.

Form three groups. Each group will take one of the items the leader has collected. Note what each item represents.
- baby doll—your boss's daughter
- play money—all the company's assets
- ball cap—a magic hat that gives the wearer the ability to sing fabulously

Then pretend that your boss has entrusted that item to you and has asked you to manage, or steward, the item while he or she leaves town for an extended period of time. Discuss what you'll do with what you've been entrusted with.

After three or four minutes share your ideas with the rest of the group. Then discuss the following questions:

- **What would your first response be if you were really put in the position of caring for one of your boss's most prized possessions?**

- **How fair would it be for your boss to expect you to take care of his or her possessions?**

- **What do you think it means to be a steward of what God has given us?**

Study It *(45-60 minutes)*

> If you have a large group, form smaller groups of four to seven people to answer the discussion questions. Allow time at the end of the Study It section for the subgroups to report to the whole group.

1. In what ways is stewardship a spiritual discipline?

Read Deuteronomy 8:17-18 and Psalm 24:1-2.

2. What do these passages teach about the source of our wealth?

3. What is the difference between being a steward and being an owner? How does this difference in status affect how you make decisions about your resources?

4. How does practicing the discipline of good stewardship affect our relationship with God? our spirituality? our lives as Christians?

learn it
live it

Read Ecclesiastes 5:10; Mark 4:18-19; I Timothy 6:9-10; and James 5:1-6.

5. What challenges do we face as we seek to use our resources wisely?

6. Form pairs or trios and divide these passages among you. Read your verses, and note what the examples teach you about being a steward of God's resources. Then share your insights with the rest of the group.

- *Matthew 19:16-22*
- *Matthew 26:6-12*
- *Luke 21:1-4*
- *Acts 4:32-35*

Read the hymn in the margin.

7. How does this hymn epitomize the actions and attitudes of a good steward?

Take My Life

Take my life, and let it be
    consecrated, Lord, to thee.
Take my moments and my days;
    let them flow in ceaseless praise,
Let them flow in ceaseless praise.

Take my hands, and let them move
    at the impulse of thy love.
Take my feet, and let them be swift
    and beautiful for thee,
Swift and beautiful for thee.

Take my voice, and let me sing,
    always, only for my King.
Take my lips, and let them be filled
    with messages from thee,
Filled with messages from thee.

Take my silver and my gold; not a
    mite would I withhold.
Take my intellect and use every
    power as thou shalt choose,
Every power as thou shalt choose.

Take my will, and make it thine; it
    shall be no longer mine.
Take my heart, it is thine own, it shall
    be thy royal throne,
It shall be thy royal throne.

Take my love; my Lord, I pour at thy
    feet its treasure store.
Take myself, and I will be ever, only,
    all for thee,
Ever, only, all for thee.

Read Matthew 25:14-30.

8. What qualities does God value in a steward?

9. What does a good steward do and think? Why does a good steward do and think these things? What is a good steward's goal?

10. What can you do to practice the spiritual discipline of stewardship better?

Close It *(15-30 minutes)*

Review the options in the Live It section of this session, and make plans as a group to complete one of these activities before you move onto the next session. This is your opportunity to move from theory to practice—*carpe diem!*

Pray It

Share prayer requests and close in prayer. Be sure to ask God to guide your efforts as you plan and carry out a Live It activity.

Plan It

What activity are we going to do?

When are we going to do this?

Where will this activity take place?

Other: Specific instructions/my responsibility

Option 1

Take an offering in your group on the day you do this Bible study on stewardship. Then decide together how you can use the money to invest in God's kingdom. Perhaps you'll spend the money on evangelism supplies and will then share the gospel in your neighborhood. Perhaps you'll use the money to adopt a child through a Christian relief agency. Perhaps you'll use the money to send a teenager to Christian camp. As you discuss what you'll spend the money on, be sure to consider what will have the most lasting effect. After you've made a decision, carry out your plans.

Option 2

As a group, decide on an amount of money each group member will invest in the kingdom of God this week. Your group might decide on ten dollars, twenty dollars, or even fifty dollars. Have each person decide individually how to spend the specified amount and then keep track of what happens as a result of the investment. At the end of the week, get together and discuss how each person spent the money and what happened.

Option 3

Spend one day this week considering how you spend your time, what you think about, what you spend money on, and how you use resources such as your home, your vehicle, and your hobby equipment. Throughout the day, ask yourself, "Am I using this as if it belonged to me or as if it were entrusted to me by God?" At the end of the day, consider how you might want to change your habits. Spend the rest of the week actively stewarding all your resources. Be ready to tell the group the discoveries and changes you made.

Option 4

Spend an hour in prayer together, asking God to show you how he would like you to use your time and resources for his glory.

God may have a project for your group to do together. Ask God to give you open ears and hearts willing to do whatever he asks you to do. Then discuss what each group member feels the group should do. You may find that God wants you to spend time serving others, giving money regularly as a group, encouraging others, sharing the gospel with others, worshipping God, or planting a new church. After your group has discussed what God has said to you, be sure to make plans immediately and carry them out.

Option 5

Meet one night to talk about financial stewardship. (Make a commitment to each other that everything shared is confidential.) Individuals or couples should come to the meeting prepared to talk about what percentages of their personal or family budgets are allocated for savings, giving, debt, and expenses. Consider how each person can best steward his or her resources. Be prepared to tell the group how decisions you've made about your budget have affected your spiritual walk. At the end of the evening, set financial goals together. Make it a goal to help one another keep your commitments to God. Set a date in the future to talk about how decisions made during this discussion have affected your spiritual life.

Debrief It

After experiencing this session's Live It activity, discuss these questions as a group:

- **On a scale of 1 (low) to 10 (high), how would you rank this experience? Why?**

- **What was the most important insight you gained from this experience?**

- **How can you incorporate this spiritual discipline into your life regularly?**

Journal It

The following space is provided for you to record your personal thoughts, reflections, impressions, or feelings about this session's topic and Live It activity.

Worship

Worship—derived from Middle English words meaning roughly "worth" and "shape" or "form"—is not about us or our preferences. It is about honoring the power, majesty, and awesome depth of the Creator of the universe and the Lover of our souls.

Both the Old and New Testaments offer wisdom for worship. The most common Hebrew word translated "worship" means to bow down. Even though the corporate worship of the Old Testament was place-oriented, with worshippers going to some particular place to bow down to God, it was meant to connect with the personal worship lived at home and in the public arena (Deuteronomy 4:5-14).

The New Testament words most commonly translated as "worship" are *proskuneo,* which means to kiss toward, and *latreuo,* which means to do the service. These are lifestyle words describing actions that are performed by individuals. The New Testament encourages worshippers to meet together (Hebrews 10:23-25) and to engage together in many of the same activities that were practiced by the faithful in the Old Testament. While Old Testament worship often focused on looking back in awe, New Testament worship often focused on encouragement to press on toward our call in Christ. Both are important elements of a flourishing worship life.

This lesson will give you the chance to study the Scriptures and take a careful look at the spiritual discipline of worship. Through study and practice, you'll learn how you can engage in personal and corporate worship in a way that nurtures and renews your focus on the one who desires to be Lord of all.

Part 1: *learn it*

Start It *(15 minutes)*

The Art of Worship

> Leader: Consider doing this session by candlelight. You may also want to play quiet worship music, such as instrumental hymn arrangements or Gregorian chants, in the background.

Recall a meaningful worship experience you've had, giving particular attention to the sights, sounds, smells, and feelings you remember. Tell the group about your experience.

When everyone has shared, discuss these questions:

- **What is worship?**

- **Is worship primarily a solitary act or a corporate act? Explain.**

- **What are the elements of a meaningful or satisfying worship experience?**

Study It *(45-60 minutes)*

> If you have a large group, form smaller groups of four to seven people to answer the discussion questions. Allow time at the end of the Study It section for the smaller groups to report to the whole group.

1. In what ways is worship a spiritual discipline?

*Take five minutes to peruse the book of Psalms
looking for verses to help you answer the next
question. Each group member should read aloud
the verses he or she discovers.*

2. Why do Christians worship God? In what ways is being a
   Christian synonymous with being a worshipper?

*Read the margin note and look up each of
the Scriptures mentioned.*

3. In practical terms, how do we worship God?
   Be as specific and complete as possible.

Robert Banks and R. Paul Stevens in *The Complete Book of Everyday Christianity* present the idea that our earthly worship should be inspired by worship that is already going on in heaven. According to Revelation, heavenly worship is responsive (3:20), reverent (4:9-10), and inclusive (5:11-14, 14:6-7). It is also intelligent, based on thinking about the qualities and actions of God (4:8, 11). "Worship in this life," wrote Banks and Stevens, "is like one grand rehearsal for the real thing...we do not keep the discipline of worship; worship keeps us."

4. How does one live out the discipline of worship every day?

5. How does worshipping God affect our lives? our relationship with God? our spirituality?

6. Why do Christians have trouble incorporating worship into everyday life?

7. Form pairs or trios and divide these passages among you. Read your verses, and note what you learn about worship. After a few minutes, summarize your verses, and share your insights with the entire group.

- I Chronicles 15:25–16:36
- Nehemiah 8:5-12; 9:1-5a
- Isaiah 6:1-8
- Mark 7:5-13

- Luke 2:21-38
- John 4:20-24
- Hebrews 10:19-25

8. How have you seen these principles of worship reflected in your own experience?

9. Does your Bible study group worship together enough? Explain. How does worship affect group life? How does private worship affect group worship and group life?

10. What can you do to practice the spiritual discipline of worship better?

Close It *(15-30 minutes)*

Review the options in the Live It section of this session, and make plans as a group to complete one of these activities prior to moving onto the next session. This is your opportunity to move from theory to practice—*carpe diem!*

Pray It

Share prayer requests and close in prayer. Be sure to ask God to guide your efforts as you plan and carry out a Live It activity.

Plan It

What activity are we going to do?

When are we going to do this?

Where will this activity take place?

Other: Specific instructions/my responsibility

Option 1

Each day this week, approach your devotional time with a sense of worshipful expectancy. Too often we approach our time with God as an opportunity to learn something, to work out our problems, to discern his will for our lives, or to receive help. This week, make it your desire to simply encounter God and to worship and minister to him with a sense of reverence, awe, and devotion. Contemplate his goodness. Praise his excellent deeds. Lift your heart to him. At the end of the week, be ready to tell the rest of the group about your time with God.

Option 2

Choose one day this week to attune yourself to God's presence. Spend the entire day, from the moment you wake until you fall asleep again, worshipping God with your thoughts, your words, your prayers, your actions, and your attitude. Whether your day is spent running errands, doing chores, working at the office, studying at school, or even enjoying a day off, worship God by doing your tasks "as unto him." Be ready to tell the rest of the group about your experience.

Option 3

Talk together about how your church typically worships. What elements are traditional in your church? What elements of worship would be out of place in your church? Make a list of ways to worship that your church does not usually practice. Then pick several of them and do them together. Be sure not to pick any mode of worship that you feel is unbiblical or that would go against the teaching of your church. Rather, choose worship modes that are simply different from what you're used to. For example, if your church only sings choruses with the words projected on the wall, sing hymns out of the hymnbook and sing the parts if you are able to. If your church doesn't use the traditional creeds, consider reciting aloud the Nicene or the Apostles' Creed. Consider how you might pray together, sing together, experience God's Word together, and celebrate communion together. Be sure to cultivate a spirit of reverence and awe during this activity. Enter fully into worshipping God together.

Option 4

Create a worship service that addresses the elements of heavenly worship described by Banks and Stevens. Decide whether you'd like to include other elements of worship based on images of worship found in the book of Revelation. Choose a time to carry out this heaven-inspired worship event, and decide if you'd like to invite others to participate with you. Plan to celebrate with a meal afterward, as many in the early church did.

Option 5

Together, plan to attend a worship service or Bible study at a church that incorporates different worship traditions than your congregation does. Arrange with leaders of the other church to go and to sit as a group, explaining that you'd like to break out of your mold for worship and to learn from the sister congregation. Commit to one another to participate as fully in the worship as you can. Consider inviting the other church to return your visit at a later date.

Debrief It

After experiencing this session's Live It activity, discuss these questions as a group:

- **On a scale of 1 (low) to 10 (high), how would you rank this experience? Why?**

- **What was the most important insight you gained from this experience?**

- **How can you incorporate this spiritual discipline into your life regularly?**

Journal It

The following space is provided for you to record your personal thoughts, reflections, impressions, or feelings about this session's topic and Live It activity.

Rest

Rest is a gift from God. However, it is a gift that we frequently do not bother to unwrap as we rush through our lives. At times, we wear our haggardness and hurriedness as a badge. But the coffeepot is a poor substitute for renewal.

Rest is more than leisure and amusement. Rest is more than just taking time off from our responsibilities. Rest is a discipline: It *is* one of our responsibilities. When God commanded us to rest, he did so for our own good. God knows our limits, so when God went about his first recorded week of work, he ended it with rest—not because he was tired, but, in part, to give us an example of how we are to live. God designed us to rest and to work. We regularly need to pull back from the demands of the day and renew ourselves.

When we neglect rest, we become brittle. We have a harder time functioning spiritually. However, when we take the time to stop, relax, enjoy, sleep—our world becomes that much brighter, and it's that much easier to exude a Christlike attitude. Your small group will benefit from discovering what the Bible has to say about rest. As you study and practice the discipline of rest as a group and as individuals, you will experience God's grace and refreshment.

Part 1:  *learn it*

Start It *(15 minutes)*
Out of Breath

> If you have a large group, form smaller groups of four to seven people and do this hands-on activity in each subgroup. Then gather to discuss the questions in the large group.

> Leader: Before the session, purchase a bag of long tube socks and roll each one individually into a ball. You'll also need a marker.

Together, brainstorm a list of demands that occupy your time on a regular basis. Use a marker to write your ideas on the socks—one idea to a sock.

Have your group sit in a circle and attempt to keep all of the socks in the air for three minutes. Pass the socks back and forth to each other. If a sock hits the floor, quickly pick it up and get it back in play.

Then discuss the following questions:

- **How is this activity like trying to keep up with life's demands?**

- **How easy is it for you to carve out time for refreshment?**

- **Why do you think rest is included in a Bible study of spiritual disciplines?**

Study It *(45-60 minutes)*

> If you have a large group, form smaller groups of four to seven people to answer the discussion questions. Allow time at the end of the Study It section for the subgroups to report to the whole group.

Read the margin quote.

1. Why do we tend to cram so much into our lives that there is so little margin for error? What are the results of this lifestyle?

Read the margin note.

2. What is rest? How does rest benefit us? How does rest affect our spirituality? our relationship with God?

In Scripture, *rest* is used to mean several different things:
• the seventh day of Creation when God rested (Genesis 2:2)
• the Sabbath, which weekly commemorates the seventh day of Creation (Exodus 20:10-11)
• the Promised Land (Deuteronomy 12:8-10)
• the peace with God that we can now have because of Christ's sacrificial death (Hebrews 4:1-3)
• our future life in heaven (Revelation 14:13)

3. What is the difference between amusement and rest? Are both beneficial? Why or why not?

Read Psalm 39:6; Psalm 55:4-8; Isaiah 28:11-13; and Isaiah 57:20-21.

4. What keeps us from experiencing God's rest?

5. Form pairs or trios. Divide the verses among the subgroups. Read the verses and discuss what they have to do with rest. After a couple of minutes, have pairs or trios summarize their verses and share their insights with the rest of the group.

- *Genesis 2:1-3*
- *Exodus 20:8-10; 31:12-13, 17*
- *Psalm 62:1, 5*
- *Isaiah 30:15; 56:2*
- *Matthew 11:28-30*
- *Hebrews 4:9-11*

Read the quotation from Leonard Sweet.

6. Why is resting spiritual?

> "The word *spirituality* comes from the Latin *spiritus,* which means 'breath of life.' In Hebrew it is *ruah;* in Greek, *pnuema;* in English, *wind* or *breath.* A 'spiritual' life is one that breathes in and out the 'breath of life.'…The root of Sabbath means 'to catch one's breath.' "
>
> **Leonard Sweet,**
> ***Soul Salsa***

7. In what ways is rest a discipline?

8. How does one practice the discipline of rest?

9. What are the challenges that you face in trying to build times of rest into your life?

10. What steps can you take to practice the spiritual discipline of rest better? How might these steps affect your life?

Close It (15-30 minutes)

Review the options in the Live It section of this session and make plans as a group to complete one of these activities. This is your opportunity to move from theory to practice—carpe diem! Since this is the last session in this study, discuss what the group would like to do next. You may want to have a party to celebrate the completion of this course.

Pray It

Share prayer requests and close in prayer. Be sure to ask God to guide your efforts as you plan and carry out a Live It activity.

Plan It

What activity are we going to do?

When are we going to do this?

Where will this activity take place?

Other: Specific instructions/my responsibility

Part 2: live it

Option 1

As a group, plan a fun, restful, all-day outing. Your only goal should be to play and have a good time, so make sure that whatever you decide to do is fun for everyone. Choose an outing that is truly restful, where people can slow down and relax. For example, plan to spend a day at the beach rather than a day at the drag races, or plan a picnic and a walk along a country lane rather than a trip to an amusement park. Make it a day to guard the senses rather than to stimulate them artificially. Enjoy one another's company, good food, and quiet conversation. As individuals, take note of how you feel during and after the outing. Plan to get together as group later to discuss the benefits of taking time for simple recreation.

Option 2

As a group, commit to getting *at least* eight hours of sleep each night for a week, and have everyone plan to spend the hour before sleep restfully in prayer, with a spiritually uplifting book, or in quiet conversation. Make sure the television, stereo, and computer are turned off. If possible, plan a gentle awakening for the mornings; for example, individuals might want to turn off their alarms or tune their clock radios to quiet, classical music. Discuss your strategies for taking care of responsibilities efficiently so that you can truly rest for at least nine hours each day. As individuals, keep a daily journal of your experiences and attitudes. At the end of the week, take note of how purposefully taking adequate rest has affected your life.

Option 3

For one week, exchange an hour that you would normally spend watching television or reading with an extra hour spent quietly with God each day. Take notes about what God is teaching you. Be prepared to share your findings from your extra rest time with your small group.

Option 4

Plan to go on a spiritual retreat together. You may find a monastery, abbey, or Christian retreat center in your area that organizes one-day spiritual retreats. If there's nothing like that in your area, organize your own spiritual retreat. You may want to go to a state or national park. Or you may simply want to plan for an overnight trip to a local country inn. Go someplace together where you can enjoy God's creation and spending time together. Plan for restful activities, such as meditating, reading, or walking. Begin and end your day with corporate prayer. You may want each person in the group to prepare a short devotion to do with the group at intervals throughout the day.

Option 5

As a group, decide to observe the Sabbath very strictly. Commit to preparing all of your meals the day before. After going to church, come straight home (no side trips to the mall or the grocery store), and take the rest of the day off. Unplug your telephone. Don't watch television, listen to the radio, or do any chores or work. Spend some extra time with God. Do whatever is most restful for you: Take a nap, go for a walk, or read the entire newspaper. Be prepared to talk about your experience at your next small group meeting.

> Note: Be mindful of your church's teachings and doctrines about the Sabbath. Some Christian traditions emphasize the need to observe a Sabbath day strictly, while other traditions hold that a strict Sabbath is no longer required for Christians. If you are not clear about the teachings of your church, ask your pastor for clarification. If your group is made up of people from more than one church, take a moment to ask the members what their churches teach about observing a day of rest. Instead of trying to mediate a disagreement, focus on finding the principles about biblical rest on which everyone can agree.

Debrief It

After experiencing this session's Live It activity, discuss these questions as a group:

- **On a scale of 1 (low) to 10 (high), how would you rank this experience? Why?**

- **What was the most important insight you gained from this experience?**

- **How can you incorporate this spiritual discipline into your life regularly?**

Journal It

The following space is provided for you to record your personal thoughts, reflections, impressions, or feelings about this session's topic and Live It activity.